COMPOSER SHOWCASE
HAL LEONARD STUDENT PIANO LIBRARY

M000166892

Jazz Bits and Pieces

ORIGINAL PIANO SOLOS IN VARIOUS JAZZ STYLES

BY BILL BOYD

CONTENTS

ISBN 0-7935-2784-8

HAL•LEONARD®
CORPORATION
7777 W. BLUEMOUND RD. P.O. BOX 13819 MILWAUKEE, WI 53213

Visit Hal Leonard Online at
www.halleonard.com

Foreword

The compositions in this book were written to introduce students to various jazz styles.

- *Over Easy* represents the swing style, and the harmonies of *Easy Over* suggest a bit of dixieland jazz.

- *Rock-a-Bye's* chord progressions make it a slow-rock ballad.

- The melodic line of *Jazz Waltz* creates a blues feeling in three-four time.

- *Swing Ding* illustrates a typical left-hand bass pattern common to the swing era.

- *What's Up?* is a faster pop-rock composition.

- *True Blues* captures the "true" blues sound without the use of the twelve-bar-blues chord progression.

- Every collection of jazz pieces must contain at least one example of the basic twelve-bar-blues chord progression... thus... *"Must Do" Blues*, in rock style.

- The rhythms and sounds of Scott Joplin appear in *Ragtime*.

- *Minor à la Mode* jazzes it up in a minor key.

- And finally, students will experience the sounds of extended and altered chords in *Chordially Yours*. Many of the possibilities exist here: raised and lowered fifths and ninths, major-seventh, and added-ninth chords.

-Bill Boyd

INTRODUCTION

The compositions in this book are written in several jazz styles . . . . rock, swing, blues and jazz waltz. Each style requires a certain type of eighth note interpretation. Generally, slow ballads, rock and pieces in six eight time are played with even eighth notes as in classical music. Uneven eighth notes are played in swing and modern jazz compositions. A more precise explanation of eighth note performance appears in the box below.

PERFORMANCE NOTES

When a practice rhythm appears at the top of a composition, play the rhythm on one note while counting out loud; then, find the measure or measures that contain the rhythm and play the actual notes.

SWING EIGHTH NOTES

Eighth notes in swing style jazz are written evenly as in classical music but are played **unevenly**. Practice the following exercises to learn the proper performance of swing eighth notes.

Play and count eighth note triplets.

Tie the first two notes of the triplet together. The resulting rhythm is the swing eighth note feeling.

The triplet rhythm with the first two notes tied together may also be notated in the following manner.

Once the swing eighth note "feeling" is achieved, the counting may revert back to "one and two and etc."

On your music, you'll see the following indication:

ROCK EIGHTH NOTES

In the rock or slow ballad styles, the notes are played evenly as in classical music.

On your music, you'll see the following indication:

OVER EASY

BILL BOYD

Commissioned by Clavier

EASY OVER

BILL BOYD

ROCK-A-BYE

BILL BOYD

JAZZ WALTZ

BILL BOYD

SWING DING

BILL BOYD

WHAT'S UP?

BILL BOYD

TRUE BLUES

BILL BOYD

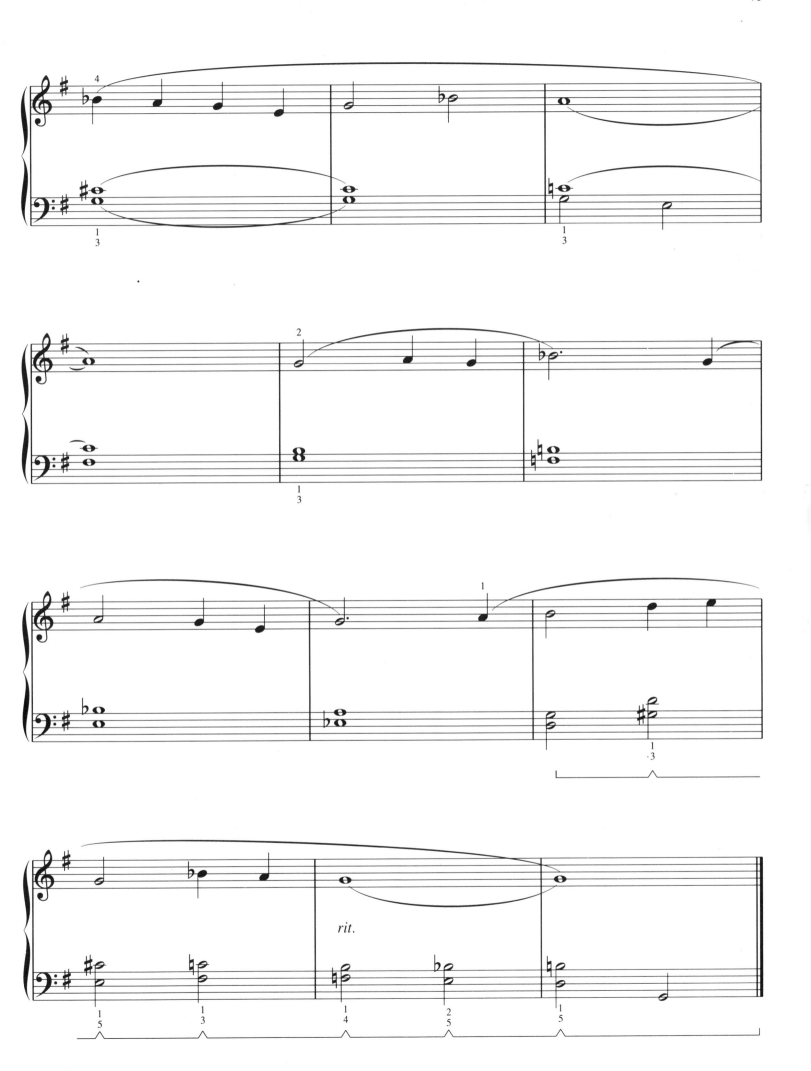

Commissioned by *Clavier*

"MUST DO" BLUES

BILL BOYD

RAGTIME

BILL BOYD

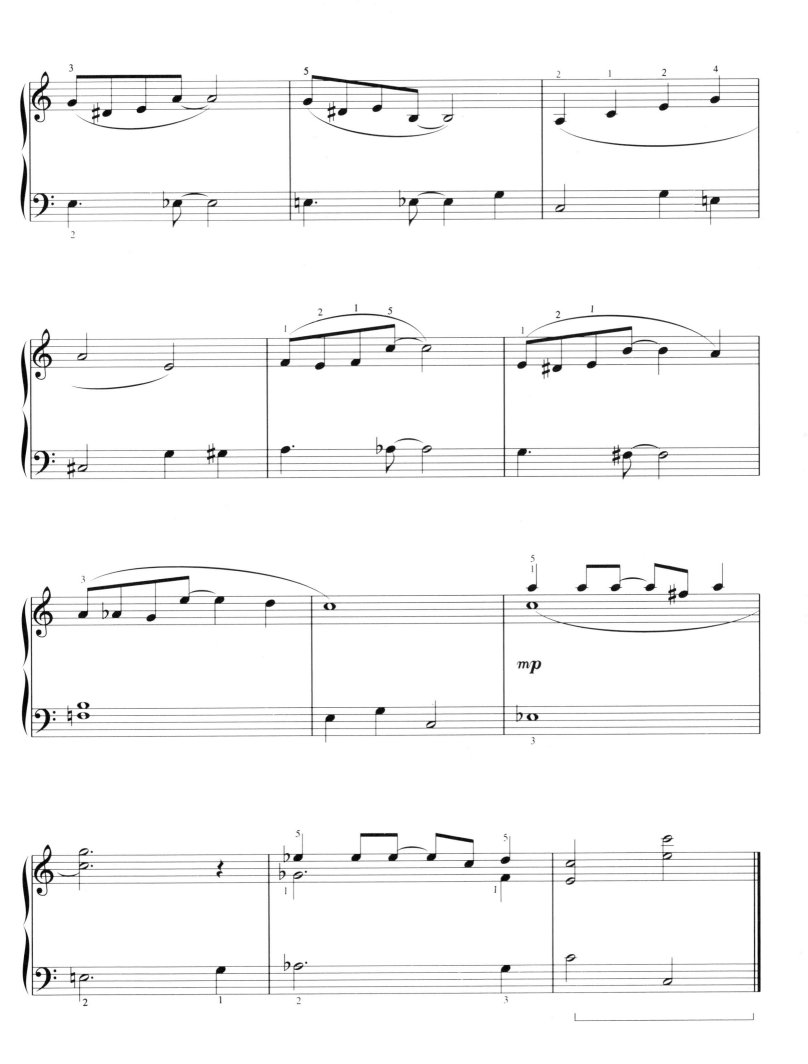

MINOR A LA MODE

BILL BOYD

CHORDIALLY YOURS

BILL BOYD

Moderately

With Pedal

mf

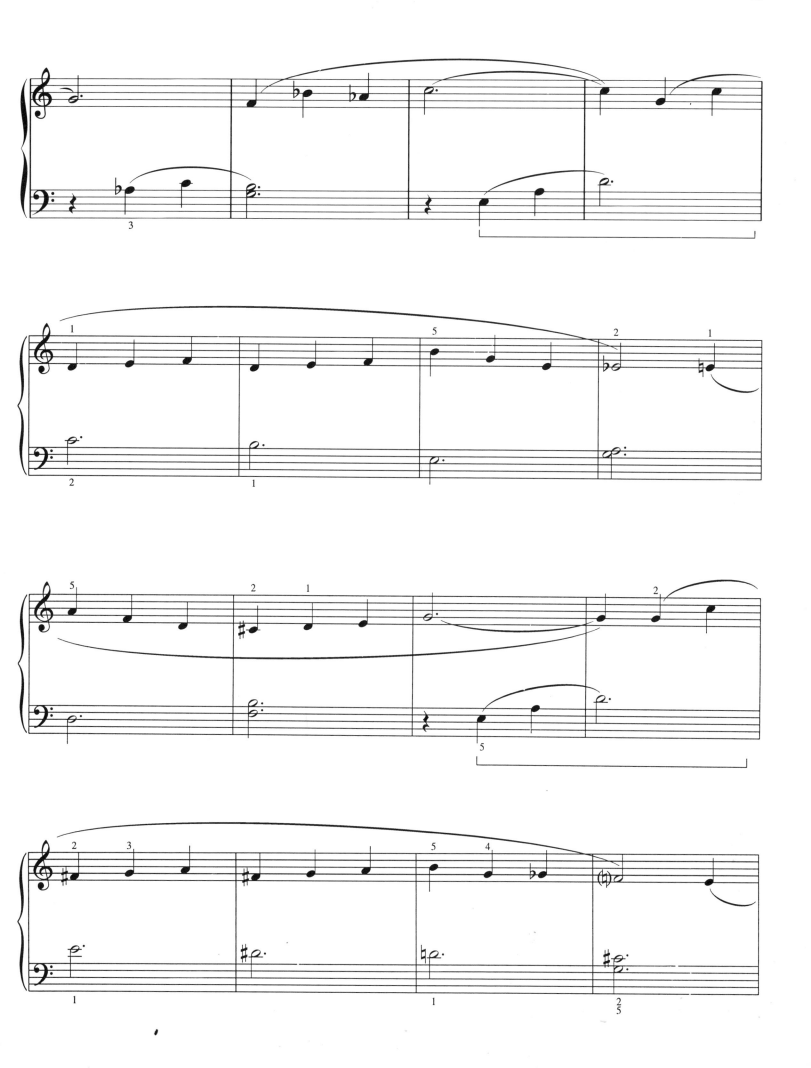

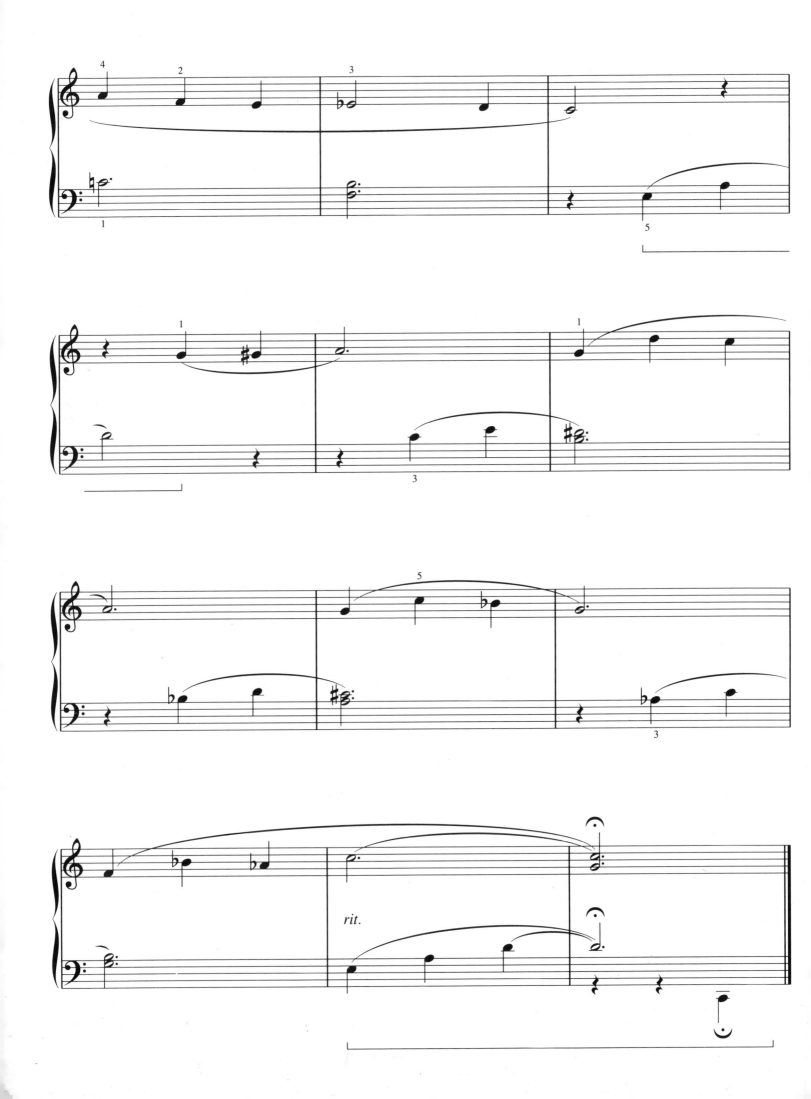